Paul Madden

RAFFLES:
Lessons in Business Leadership

CW01335624

WhosWho Publishing

Text Copyright © Paul Madden
Cartoons Copyright © Ang Lee Ming

First published 2003

WhosWho Publishing
an imprint of WhosWho Pte Ltd
20 Upper Circular Road, #12-03
Singapore 058416
Tel: +65 6538 5635

All rights reserved. No part of this publication may
be reproduced, stored in a retrieval system, or
transmitted, in any form or by any means, electronic,
mechanical, photocopying, recording or otherwise,
without the prior permission of the publishers.

ISBN 981-4062-00-6

Set in Times pt 12 by WhosWho Publishing
Printed in Singapore by COS Printers Pte Ltd

For Sarah

embodiment of Lesson 18

Acknowledgements

The idea for this book grew out of a talk I was asked to give at the AGM of the British Chamber of Commerce in Singapore, just as I was completing my MBA thesis. Afterwards some friends suggested that I write it up.

I would like to pay tribute to Susan Wakeford, literary agent; Ang Lee Ming who drew the amusing cartoons; and to Low Kar Tiang, my excellent publisher who became a friend, who harried, cajoled and encouraged me to ensure that we ended up with a much better product than would otherwise have been possible.

I am grateful to Neil Montefiore, CEO of M1, for his personal encouragement, and for M1's generous sponsorship which made this publication possible.

I would like to thank my parents for their encouragement, and my children, Sebastian, Rupert and Francesca, for their tolerance. Above all, I would like to thank my wife, Sarah, for being friend, confidante and the pillar of support which makes everything else possible.

Paul Madden
Singapore
May 2003

Foreword

My first encounter with *Raffles: Lessons in Business Leadership* was at the British Chamber of Commerce when I attended a presentation by my good friend, Paul Madden. It turned out to be as fascinating as it was instructive. The life of a hitherto remote historical figure, albeit a Singapore icon, became meaningful to me in a completely unexpected way!

What Paul had to say about the leadership style of Sir Stamford Raffles and his relevance to modern management methods gave me a refreshingly new perspective of the founder of Singapore. I knew instinctively that Paul's incisive study had an appeal that went beyond the confines of the room that day and that it deserved a much larger audience for the insights it could impart. I suggested to Paul that he should consider turning the presentation into a book. I am extremely glad that he did.

Raffles: Lessons in Business Leadership will, no doubt, make a very interesting and beneficial read for many corporate executives and business students in Singapore. Already au fait with the works of popular management gurus of the day, they are likely to discover a new dimension to the management principles according to Sir Stamford Raffles. Principles which appear to have been validated after the passage of some 180 years! I say this with due respect and without taking anything away from the likes of Peter Drucker, Kenneth Blanchard and Tom Peters.

The achievements and indeed also some of the failings of Sir Stamford Raffles the colonial administrator, entrepreneur and scholar have been cleverly distilled into 20 convenient nuggets of management wisdom in this highly readable book. Each relates to a particular episode in his life and work and draws a specific lesson on some of the best practices of modern management. Aspiring managers and business leaders will do well to take heed of these lessons and to put them into practice, adapting where necessary.

I see *Raffles: Lessons in Business Leadership* making a useful and significant contribution to Singapore literature in a wider sense; it will help connect Singaporeans and Singapore's founder at another level.

Many of us, I suspect, have regarded Sir Stamford Raffles as an important historical figure but perhaps rather obscure and totally irrelevant to life in Singapore in the 21st century. We can now look at him in another light; as a dynamic and skilful leader in the business and politics of his time who speaks to us over a span of almost two centuries and makes perfect sense!

Paul Madden, I believe, has succeeded in opening our eyes and minds to our past for invaluable lessons that will help us manage our present and our future.

Neil Montefiore
Chief Executive Officer
MobileOne Ltd

CONTENTS

INTRODUCTION

Sir Stamford Raffles, founder of Singapore. Entrepreneur, scholar, colonial administrator. His name graces many enterprises around the City State today, from schools to hotels and major corporations. In Singapore's colonial district his statues stand outside the Victoria Theatre and on Boat Quay. In London his portrait hangs in the National Portrait Gallery, and his statue can be found in Westminster Abbey.

We all feel we know him. But there are many parts of his story which have escaped popular attention. He was a study in contrasts. The dynamic man of action who loved nothing better than quiet study. The popular leader who accumulated well-placed patrons and bitter enemies in equal measure.

Even the name was changed. To his family and friends, Raffles was Tom, the name with which he had been christened. It was only when knighted at the age of 35 that he took on his middle name, the rather grander Stamford, for public use.

There is some debate about the extent to which Raffles should be credited with founding modern Singapore. After all, he spent less than eleven months in the place in total. Certainly Singapore owes much to his immediate subordinates Farquhar and Crawford, who played such a prominent role in establishing the foundations of the infant colony.

But Raffles deserves the credit for his vision in making the decisive move to establish the new port in the Straits in 1819.

History has been rather kinder to Raffles than life itself was. Despite achieving prominence in his own times, it was in many ways a life of tragedy. His family was destroyed by tropical diseases and his career left in tatters by a series of bitter feuds.

But Raffles was more than just another 19th century colonial figure. Nearly 200 years on, his life, including its successes and failures, holds many lessons for today's business leaders. Particularly those working in the international business arena as expatriate managers, or mobile executives.

Was he a businessman or a bureaucrat? The answer is something of each, reflecting the complex nature of his employer, the English East India Company – one of the world's first multinational corporations.

But in either case, he was certainly a leader. One who had a profound impact on the people he worked with. And one who proved the catalyst for the achievement of great things. What can we learn from his character and the way he exercised his leadership?

This book begins with a brief account of Raffles' life. It then sets the context by describing, in business terms, the organisation for which he worked – the East India Company, and the market place in which he operated. It analyses his behaviour as a leader, and then attempts to distil a series of specific lessons which are directly relevant to today's business world.

Raffles lived between 1781 and 1826. A period during which the mystical East began to become properly part of an integrated world market system for western business adventurers. It also marked the start of the translation of the scientific revolution into an industrial revolution which would drive business and trade during the Victorian era. It was a time of flux and opportunity. In short, it was a time like today.

A BRIEF SKETCH OF RAFFLES' LIFE

Raffles' fame of course stems from his achievement in the founding of Singapore. But in fact it occupied only a relatively small part of his relatively short life. In total he spent only eleven months in Singapore, in three visits over a period of four years.

Much of his current renown results from the subsequent success of Singapore after his death. But Singapore's story owes much to Raffles' original blinding insight into the opportunities which its location offered, and to the drive with which he pursued them.

Although he had achieved power in the Far East and celebrity at home, by the time of his death, in Hendon, north London, in 1826, he was neglected, almost bankrupt and had already buried four of his five children.

Both his successes and his failures result from a driven personality. We can all profit from the lessons which they offer.

Raffles was born in 1781 on board his father's ship in the Caribbean. Financial necessity put him early to work at the age of 14 as a clerk in the East India Company in London.

After 10 years slaving away for a pittance, combined with long hours of study at night to make up for his lost education, he was offered a post in Penang. The rewards of an expatriate package were as good then as now. His salary shot up from £79 to £1,500. On the strength of his new found affluence, he married Olivia and set off for the mysterious East.

Energy, acumen and diligence in his Malay studies brought steady advancement in Penang and subsequently Malacca.

Meanwhile back at home, the Napoleonic wars were in full flow. When France's annexation of the Netherlands created a temporary power vacuum in their eastern colonies, Raffles joined an 1811 mission to take over Java, led by the Governor General of India, Lord Minto. His potential clearly impressed Minto, who appointed him Lieutenant Governor to stay on and administer the new territory.

Raffles was a competent, at times visionary, administrator in Java, but not a great financial success. When the colony was handed back to the Dutch in 1816 after the French were defeated, he travelled back to London for 16 months.

In London, his colonial exploits and his geographic and scientific achievements won great acclaim. He was lionised by London society, acquired new patrons and returned to the East to take up a new appointment as Lieutenant Governor of Bencoolen in Sumatra, with a new wife Sophia (Olivia having died in 1814) and a knighthood.

Concerned that Dutch dominance of the archipelago aimed to monopolise the China trade and ultimately drive out the British, he lobbied vociferously for a UK settlement in a more strategic location than Penang.

Stretching his masters' instructions for an exploratory mission to the Riau Islands, well beyond their original intent, he signed a treaty with the native rulers and founded Singapore in 1819. His superiors acquiesced somewhat reluctantly, conscious that this act of aggrandisement risked provoking the Dutch into renewed hostilities.

Over the next four years, Raffles oversaw Singapore from the distance of his lieutenant governorship of Bencoolen. His detailed instructions laid the foundations for much of Singapore's subsequent success, although he spent less than a year there in total.

By the time he sailed home from the East in 1824, Singapore was already a fast-growing commercial success.

It was not exactly a triumphal return home. Raffles survived a fire which sunk the *Fame*, the ship he was returning on, and destroyed much of his fortune and his treasure trove of Malayan artefacts and literature. The fire was allegedly caused by a drunken sailor opening a barrel of highly inflammable brandy with a naked candle in his hands. They engaged another ship, but that was unable to sail when the captain suddenly went stark raving mad.

He eventually got back to London, only to face niggling disputes with his employer. In essence they claimed he had fiddled his expenses. How many businessmen today can relate to that? But he still found time to participate in the London social scene, as well as founding London Zoo.

He died in July 1826 at the age of 45 from a brain tumour which had kept him in growing ill health for a number of years, leaving his wife saddled with debts.

But despite the sad ending, it was by no means a life of failure. Raffles' vision in founding Singapore was to be vindicated time and again over the next 200 years or so. Already, within eight years of his death, his stock had risen sufficiently for his statue to be placed in Westminster Abbey, amidst the pantheon of British achievement.

THE COMPANY

What sort of organisation did Raffles work for? Was it a private sector multinational or an arm of government? Was it, in modern Singaporean terms, a Government Linked Company (GLC)? The answer is not straightforward. The business model of the English East India Company changed over time, and operated in different ways in different places.

It had been founded by Royal Charter on 31 December 1600 as "The Company of Merchants of London trading into the East Indies". Today's branding consultants would no doubt suggest a slightly snappier title. Some writers have described it as a sort of halfway house between the medieval guild and the modern public limited company.

Domestically, it had a clear run at its market. To reduce some of the risks of what was a very high risk start-up, the Charter granted a 15-year monopoly of eastern trade. In 1609 this had been made permanent.

Initially each voyage was funded independently. But in 1613 the finances were put on a sounder long term footing, by issuing a joint stock, through which backers invested in a fleet a year for four years. Following the model developed a little earlier by the Dutch East India Company, this was a very important step in business organisation.

From the start the business model was very much import driven. The Company was seeking foreign products and commodities to ship back to the London markets, rather than pursuing export opportunities for Britain's nascent manufacturing industry. Over time the geographical focus switched. First pepper from the East Indies, then cotton from India, and finally tea from China.

Modern business managers frequently find themselves

asking – what business are we in? By Raffles' time this was a very apt question for the Company. Essentially there were two very diverse, but interconnected business groups, with quite different organisational structures and revenue streams.

On the Indian subcontinent, the focus had shifted from trade to administration of territories. The Company's income came from tax revenues, not trading profits. Its staff had become civil servants more than merchants. Further east, on the other hand, the China business was much more of a traditional international trading operation, based on shipping and a network of far-flung trading posts.

Nowadays, consultants frequently recommend demerger and the hiving-off of activities, when the disparate elements of a large conglomerate become so different from each other that they bring into question where the business' core competences really lie. The East India Company managers were well aware of this contradiction. Surely, they argued, the government should take over the administration of the Indian territories. Yes, they actually wanted part of the business to be nationalised!

But the British government was having enough trouble with its American colonies. It resisted the temptation to take on a new set of problems in India. It did however pass Acts in 1773 and 1785 which increasingly brought government influence to bear on the management of the East India Company. The CEO slot, or Governor General as he was called, became a Royal appointment, and government ministers, including a Secretary of State for India, sat on the Company's supervisory Board of Control.

The government aimed to stay clear of the strictly trading activities. But it did deliver the Company a major commercial advantage by slashing the duty on tea imports. This more than made up for any loss in Indian revenue. The decision was certainly vindicated by the huge growth in tea consumption. By 1830 the British government was making £3 million a year from tea duties, a significant proportion of its total tax receipts.

The regulatory environment remained very favourable to the Company. Who wouldn't want to be a licensed monopoly? Not surprisingly, disadvantaged firms at home began to create political pressure for liberalisation. In particular, British manufacturers such as the textile producers, argued that the Company's lack of interest in exporting their products effectively denied them access to eastern markets.

The British government slowly opened up the regime. From 1793, Company ships were required to carry a certain minimum tonnage of private cargo at concessionary rates. In 1813, the India trade was opened up to competitors, and finally, in 1833, the China trade was opened.

The Company was eventually dissolved in 1858 and finally wound up in 1873. By then Raffles was long dead, and Singapore flourishing.

The original corporate structure consisted of a Court of Proprietors, representing the investors, and a Court of Committees, later the Court of Directors, comprising the senior executives.

At the local level, individual business units such as the establishments in Calcutta, Bombay, Madras and Bencoolen were known as Presidencies, each headed by a governor and his Council. In 1773 the Governor of Bengal in Calcutta was given authority over the other business units and the title of Governor General. Sounds much better than Vice President (Asian Affairs) doesn't it?

But lines of reporting were not as clear-cut in those

days. Patronage was rife, both in London and locally. Huge profits were being made in India, and Indian fortunes were being turned into political power back in London. Raffles played the patronage game assiduously, often, but not always, successfully.

To describe the picture entirely in terms of the Company's formal organisation and trading patterns is a little misleading. The Company's monopoly covered only the inward and outward voyages from Europe. Shipments within the Indies, known as "country trade", became enormously important over time. Country trade was conducted both by Company staff acting on their own account, and by "private traders" – including Company staff who had resigned and stayed out East.

Nowadays we might describe them as Small and Medium Enterprises (SMEs) spun out of a parent company. Sometimes the trade was shipped through rented space in the holds of Company ships, but an even greater volume flowed through numerous local craft like Chinese junks and Malay prahu. Huge fortunes were made.

For many Company employees, trading on their own account was a much higher priority than their work for the Company. Today's corporations would have something to say about that. Indeed the system was open to abuse, with great potential for blurring the lines between personal and Company cargo.

But it meant that the Company could get away with paying its staff less, while still attracting dynamic, entrepreneurial individuals. Private shipping often led the way into new markets and new products, which the Company could subsequently take advantage of.

When Raffles arrived in Penang, it had only just been

raised to the same legal status as the Presidencies in India. Its political and commercial clout within the business was a long way behind that of the longer established operating units in India. The whole Company was dominated by officers who had served in India.

Raffles was very unusual in starting in South East Asia straight away, without first gaining experience in India. Nor did he ever seem particularly keen to move on to India. He quickly established the archipelago as his field of operations. He determined to be a big fish in a small, but very rapidly growing pool.

THE MARKET PLACE

What was the market place in which Raffles was operating? Originally, the Indies had been a rather loose description covering everything east of the Cape of Good Hope and west of the Azores. Raffles chose to confine his specific area of activity to what we now know as South East Asia.

This had been the scene of some of the East India Company's earliest activities, in its unsuccessful attempts to muscle into a spice trade dominated by the Dutch in the early 17th century. While still a source of important commodities, by the time of Raffles, the region's importance lay more in its role in the China trade.

Trade with China was very heavily regulated by the authorities of the Celestial Kingdom. All trade was channelled through the single port of Canton (Guangzhou) on the Pearl River. Foreign vessels had to wait downstream at the Portuguese port of Macau to be processed.

A small number of foreign traders were allowed to construct "factories" (actually warehouses) on the waterfront in Canton. But they had to move back to Macau every summer when business slackened off. There were strict controls on what the Europeans could do in Canton: they could bring in no women or guns, and were forbidden to stray beyond the harbour area.

Within Canton, the Chinese end of the trade was restricted to a small number of local merchants. This cartel system, known as *co-hong*, made it easy for them to fix prices against the western traders.

These restrictions bit even more heavily on the small private traders who were becoming an increasingly significant element in the market place, in the shadow of the major multinational trading monopolies.

China was a very important source of several commodities highly prized in the West. Initially silk had been the most significant, but gradually tea came to predominate. An upmarket delicacy at first, it won mass market appeal after the 1720s when increased volumes of sugar from the West Indies became available in London.

Imports of tea grew rapidly over the next 60 years, then increased exponentially when the Commutation Act of 1784 slashed duty on tea from between 79 to 129 per cent down to just 12.5 per cent. The Company was purchasing more tea from China than all its competitors combined. No wonder Britain came to be known as a nation of tea drinkers.

Unfortunately the Chinese were rather dismissive about what the West had to offer in return. There was some limited interest in mechanical devices from Europe, and food and medicinal products from the South East Asian archipelago. But no great interest in Britain's leading export, woollen broadcloth, or indeed in Indian cottons. So for many years China ran a substantial trade surplus, paid for by large inflows of silver bullion.

In the second half of the 18th century, the East India Company devoted much effort to trying to find goods which the Chinese did want. Gradually a triangular trade developed: Indian cottons and saltpetre (used in gunpowder) were shipped to South East Asia, where they were traded for pepper and other spices, tin ore, gold dust, animal skins and delicacies like birds nests and sharks fins which could find a ready market in China.

Raffles faced a very competitive market place. The Indies was just one of several territories in which British businessmen and their global competitors fought out a fierce struggle. The challenge was of course not just commercial, but political and military. Competition was vicious both in the home markets of Europe and in the New World of the Americas. Switching alliances at home could rapidly have a significant impact on business at the other side of the world.

The Players

Let us look at some of the key players and the role they played in this market place.

In South East Asia, the Dutch were the *incumbent*, with a dominant position throughout the archipelago based on two centuries of profitable spice trade. The Dutch East India Company, or VOC, probably the world's first modern multinational corporation, was well entrenched. Their regional headquarters was located at Batavia, modern day Jakarta, in Java. Their routes to the Indies were supported by possessions in modern day South Africa and Sri Lanka.

Globally the stronger player, and with a substantial regional base in the Indian market, the English East India Company nevertheless played the role of *challenger* in Raffles' business arena.

The French Compagnie des Indes were *fellow challengers* in this market place. They had temporarily seized the Company's settlement at Bencoolen in the 1760s. They had been actively exploring the coast of Indochina, and their warships preyed on British traffic between India and China.

The Spanish had a smaller, *specialist niche* in the China trade, which they pursued through a rather different business model using different distribution channels. They competed in China from their historic base in the Philippines, supported by silver bullion shipments to Manila direct from their investments across the Pacific in Mexico and Peru.

The Portuguese were what modern marketeers would call a *legacy brand*. They still held Macau, and Goa on the west coast of India. But since 1635 these had been open to other players too. And the important Malay trading hub in Malacca had fallen to the Dutch as long ago as 1641.

It is important not to underestimate the role of *SMEs*, or small local players: Chinese, Malays and Bugis. They had been actively trading in these waters for centuries. Collectively their economic impact was substantial.

The Tactics

The tactics used by the different players would be readily recognised in the modern market environment.

1. Strategic Alliances

The prime rationale for the various strategic alliances which formed at different times, tended to be located in the European market place. But their implications for South East Asia were significant. The principal backdrop was a long-running series of wars between England and France, opportunistically extended into other battle fronts. For example, when Spain allied itself with France in 1761, the East India Company occupied and held Manila for 18 months.

More important was the alliance between the Dutch and the French. The English East India Company directors and the British government had no strategic ambitions to deprive the Dutch of their possessions in Java. But to avoid Dutch ports becoming available to French ships, it was judged tactically necessary to take them temporarily into control.

Raffles sometimes deliberately confused the tactical and strategic imperatives, failing to acknowledge that this was just a holding operation and the possessions would eventually return to Dutch ownership. As Lieutenant Governor of Java from 1811, he set in train a series of substantial reforms in the fields of agriculture, commerce and finance, and was disappointed when the territory was handed back to the Dutch after Napoleon was defeated at Waterloo.

2. Encirclement

The Company was building up its network of trading positions strung all along the route from Europe to the Indies. In particular its bridgehead in India was a strong base, both financial and military, to support its business ambitions further east.

3. Attacking on new fronts

As we have seen, the conventional model of Chinese trade through Canton was heavily weighted against the European traders. They needed to break out of this system by establishing a base outside the Chinese sphere of control, where independent Chinese junks from a range of ports, not just Canton, could come and trade.

Strategically they also needed a military base somewhere in South East Asia so that ships of the Royal Navy could protect British commerce in the South China Sea.

Both of these goals had fuelled the search for a new base in the region, and in 1786 the Company had settled on Penang on the western coast of the Malay peninsula. The settlement was further upgraded in 1805 when the Navy committed to make it a significant naval port with dockyard, and the Company increased its investment and upgraded Penang's status to a full regional HQ, or as they called it, a Presidency, like those in Calcutta, Bombay and Madras. It was this development which brought Raffles to the East.

Raffles quickly realised that Penang was in the wrong place. Too far north to tap into the archipelago's domestic trade, and the wrong side of the Malay peninsula to draw junks from China in large numbers. It was his relentless search for an alternative that ultimately led to the founding of Singapore.

4. Product innovation

Eventually the Company found a product which could find a market in China, and which they could control by exercising their monopoly producer position in India – opium. They were careful to ensure that the drug was shipped into China by private traders, since it was illegal. Nevertheless the huge expansion of opium shipments was key to the China trade.

5. Spoiling tactics

The Company was keen to take advantage of its temporary hold over Malacca, during the Anglo-French wars, to run down the Dutch city's operations in favour of Penang. They hoped its people and trade would migrate to Penang so that when it was eventually returned to Dutch control, it would be a much weaker competitor.

However, Raffles opposed this policy. His own detailed examination of trade within the region, and in particular the role played by local traders like the Bugis from Sulawesi and Borneo, suggested that Malaccan trade played an important role in the complex network on which Penang's own prosperity depended. He successfully persuaded Calcutta to change course.

6. Intellectual property

Maps and sea charts were crucial intellectual property in the sprawling archipelago. They were zealously guarded. Indeed it was industrial espionage which had allowed the Dutch to win a toe-hold in the region two centuries before, when a Dutch cartographer, Van Linshoten, copied Portuguese maps of all the eastern sea routes while serving as secretary to the Archbishop of Goa.

RAFFLES' LESSONS FOR BUSINESS LEADERS

To what extent does Raffles match up to modern ideas of what is required for business leadership? It is instructive to look at this in terms of his personality, and the way he used the various tools of successful leaders.

In essence, leadership is about influencing groups and individuals and marshalling resources to achieve specific goals. Raffles certainly met this test. He attained a number of major goals, some personal and some defined by the Company (the two were often far from the same thing). Perhaps not surprisingly, he failed to deliver a number of desired outcomes along the way too.

To achieve all this he needed to carry various groups of people with him, using a variety of leadership tools and approaches. Here the record is more patchy. While he won great loyalty from many colleagues and business partners, he made enemies too.

Raffles could certainly be described as a "type A" personality: aggressive, impatient, competitive, explosive. Though he could be very charming and persuasive too. Some commentators have suggested a "Napoleon complex" arising from his short stature. Interestingly, Raffles met the imprisoned Napoleon on the island of St Helena on his way back to England. It was not a friendly encounter. Neither man warmed to the other. Perhaps they were just too similar?

Academics have identified a number of tools available to leaders to achieve their desired ends:

1. Reward. Raffles gathered around him a coterie of friends and supporters, often family members, whom he was able to reward with minor patronage. This was very typical of the times. As Lieutenant Governor in Java, then Bencoolen,

he was also in a position to directly influence the profits which others could make, for example, from land speculation.

2. Coercion. A governor had considerable autonomy to control financial and human resources within his own territory. But Raffles did not succeed in coercing several key subordinates, like Farquhar, his deputy, in Singapore. Even when he used the ultimate sanction of sacking them, they proved able to damage him from afar afterwards. Just like today, the stick proved less effective than the carrot.

3. Charisma. This was clearly a strong point for Raffles. He was capable of charming people in a very wide range of business relationships: his immediate entourage, his admirers in Calcutta and London, native chieftains, and power brokers. He wanted people to love him, and was upset when occasionally, they did not.

4. Legitimacy. In a large bureaucracy like the East India Company, power was to a significant extent derived from one's formal position within the company hierarchy. But even in his early years in Penang, Raffles was never constrained by his junior status. He always sought to push the boundaries.

5. Expertise. From the first, Raffles' command of the Malay language was a major asset in his career. His studies into the natural environment of the region and into Malay politics made him a genuine expert, whose insights were respected and valued by superiors and subordinates alike. Through his publications he also made sure that his expertise was widely recognised.

6. Information. Knowledge is power, they say, and Raffles was often able to win the argument by weight of information. For example, his detailed study of the shipping traffic of its port played a crucial role in influencing decisions about the future of Malacca.

7. Connections. The ability of a leader to influence players across a wide network, beyond their overt power sources, can often be vital. In modern terms, Raffles had a huge pile of metaphorical business cards, which he deployed assiduously.

Of course, successful leaders use a combination of all these techniques, selecting whatever tools make best sense in specific circumstances.

The principal lessons from Raffles' life and achievements, for today's business leaders, can be divided into four main categories:

1. Market place awareness. Scanning the business environment, looking for opportunities, a commitment to the search for knowledge as a source of competitive advantage.

2. Dynamism and flexibility. The ability to act rapidly to take advantage of opportunities, to take risks, to be decisive in the short term, while retaining a clear view of the long term.

3. Working the corporate hierarchy. Raffles secured and used very effectively several highly placed patrons at regional HQ in India, and corporate HQ in London. For long periods, and in major areas, he got away with going well beyond the instructions of his superiors. But his failure to carry the system with him ultimately brought down financial ruin on his head. And although he was widely admired by most people who had personal contact with him, he had a series of bad relationships with his deputies which stoked the fires of corporate discontent.

4. Personal life. Maintaining the work-life balance and ensuring that the results are worth it.

20 lessons have been distilled from Raffles' leadership, lessons which are as relevant to business at the beginning of the 21st century as they were at the beginning of the nineteenth.

THE LESSONS

Lesson 1

Build a learning organisation

Modern multinational companies aspire to be "learning organisations", which actively gather knowledge and disseminate it through the system. They promote learning by individual employees, by the organisation as a whole and by its stakeholders. Only by a constant search for ways to do things better can they remain competitive. They recognise that the ability to learn faster than the competition may be the only long term sustainable competitive advantage.

Raffles' schooling ended at 14 when the money ran out. Like many whose early education was interrupted, he had a passion for study and a commitment to life-long learning.

During the long, dull years as a clerk in London, he burnt the midnight oil catching up with his studies. It was literally the midnight oil: there is a story of his mother complaining about the profligate use of candles which the family could ill afford. In short, he was something of a swot.

Raffles was an able, indeed highly intelligent student. By the time of his overseas posting in 1805 he spoke good French, and had acquired as good a learning in science and literature as many of his contemporaries who had received a more formal education.

The habit of study was maintained during the long voyage out to Penang. By the time he arrived there he had already tackled the rudiments of the Malay language. This singled him out among his contemporaries, gave him a head start in carrying out his business, and was a springboard for his relatively rapid promotion.

But Raffles was not content with a working knowledge of spoken and written Malay. It opened up for him a new world of opportunities for the further study of Malay history and literature, which became a life-long pursuit.

His academic leanings were given a boost by a friendship he struck up shortly after arriving in Penang. John Leyden, a brilliant Scottish scholar, who was said to know 26 languages, provided a real stimulus to Raffles' own endeavours. Leyden became close to both Raffles and Olivia, and indeed fell in love with the latter. Raffles was devastated when he died of malaria in 1811, shortly after the conquest of Java.

Raffles also liked to surround himself with scientists who shared his passion for exploration. In Java he got to know Dr Thomas Horsfield, an American naturalist and scholar of the island's flora, fauna and geology.

During his first leave in Britain in 1816-17, Raffles made the acquaintance of many luminaries of London's intellectual elite. He became a Fellow of the Royal Society. When he returned to Bencoolen after his leave in London he brought with him Dr Joseph Arnold as personal physician and naturalist.

He hired locals to track down material for him, amassing perhaps the greatest collection of Malay literature in the world at that time. Ironically, the loss of that treasury with the sinking of the *Fame* was a major setback to Malay studies.

He worked with colleagues on the production of a Malay dictionary and wrote acclaimed histories of the South East Asian region. For Raffles, the search for knowledge was a major reason for the European presence in the Indies. It was not just about trade.

The scale of this achievement is even greater when we consider the lack of manuals to assist the learning of Malay, and indeed the physical difficulties of poring over fading texts by candle light in the sweltering, non air-conditioned tropical heat of the early 19th century. His native servant Abdullah said: "He loved most to sit in quietude, when he did nothing but read and write."

Education was not ignored in Raffles' grand designs for the future development of Singapore. He planned the establishment of an institution for learning in Singapore, with three sets of objectives:
- to educate the sons of the local ruling class
- to instruct foreigners in native languages
- to collect the literature and traditions of the country.

The school's future success was far from assured. His regional HQ in Calcutta were less certain than Raffles of the need for it. Indeed it went through several permutations. But ultimately his visionary creation went on to become the prestigious and eponymous Raffles Institution which still dominates Singapore's school system today.

When he finally returned home in 1824, he helped to establish London Zoo, where his statue was placed in the Lion House, appropriately enough for the founder of Singapore, the Lion City.

Lesson 2

Actively scan the business environment

In a marketing-led organisation, environmental scanning is a key function. This involves not just a detailed scanning of the immediate market place of customers, competitors and suppliers, but a wider monitoring of political, economic, social and technological trends which could have a substantial impact on competitiveness. Raffles' combination of insatiable curiosity and relentless drive made him an early practitioner of modern market analysis techniques.

As we have already seen, Raffles was heavily engaged in a wide variety of scholarship. Partly for its own sake, because he wanted to learn and then communicate what he had discovered. But partly because of the competitive edge it could bring over rival organisations. He was interested to learn from the writings of others, and from discussions with local and western scholars. Above all, he was keen to get out and see things for himself.

He was a keen student of political, economic, social and technological trends.

1. Political trends

It was his understanding of the complex relationships between the competing rulers of the island of Singapore which enabled him to sign the treaty establishing the East India Company's initial presence on the island.

When Raffles arrived in Singapore in 1819 there were two levels of authority. The Temenggong was in local control, owing allegiance to the Sultan of Johor. Raffles learned that the incumbent Sultan, a Dutch ally, had actually usurped the title of his elder brother who had been away when their father died. By supporting the "rightful heir", Sultan Hussein, Raffles was able to sign a potentially lucrative agreement and poke the Dutch competition in the eye at the same time.

Raffles was highly attuned to wider political developments. He was very aware of the implications of the Napoleonic conflict in Europe for the various participants' colonial empires in the East.

2. Economic trends

Raffles recognised the importance of economic trends which underlay the political framework and which would drive business into new directions.

He understood the importance of the ever-growing

China trade, and its implications for the Company's interests in South East Asia. He was also keen to examine the micro-trading patterns of local cargoes carried by the native traders: where did they go and what sort of goods did they carry?

Raffles was familiar with the writings of Adam Smith, who had published his magnum opus, *The Wealth of Nations*, just four years before Raffles' birth. It would have been hard for any Englishman involved in international business not to have been aware of the arguments for free trade. This strongly shaped Raffles' thinking about the future development of Singapore.

3. Social trends

Raffles wanted to learn about Malay and other East Asian cultures, so that he could understand what made his interlocutors tick. He wanted to know about the pattern of social structures which formed the backdrop to his business.

Learning a language very different from one's own inevitably involves learning a lot about the culture which lies behind it. The hidden assumptions and thought patterns explain why people choose to express themselves in particular ways. Even in today's business world with English as the ubiquitous lingua franca, being able to speak the customer's language brings significant advantage.

Raffles was genuinely interested in the peoples of the East. Not just as a human resource to be exploited. Some became collaborators, fellow scholars, even friends.

4. Technological trends

Raffles' interest in science and technology was not just academic. As a business leader, he sought to understand the potential market in the diverse range of commodities which could be traded between the East and Europe. While in Java he promoted new products like coffee.

Moreover, the quest for scientific exploration gave him a useful excuse to explore new territories, make contact with local rulers, and discover new political and economic opportunities.

It was much easier in the early 19th century to be a man of science as well as a man of letters. The corpus of shared knowledge among educated circles was much smaller then than today. Raffles was free to dabble widely in his scientific interests.

With the guidance and encouragement of the scientists with whom he surrounded himself, he followed the scientific principle: he wanted to record his findings accurately in order to ensure their practical utility.

Raffles keenly studied the natural environment of South East Asia. He was an inveterate collector of animal and plant specimens. Imagine his delight in the discovery on Sumatra of an extraordinary new plant species, with a giant red flower a metre in diameter. The London experts who named it *Rafflesia Arnoldia*, ensured that his name and that of his collaborator, would be preserved for botanical posterity too.

Raffles' house at Bencoolen was like a zoo, well stocked with exotic animals and birds. When the *Fame* went down on his final journey back to England in 1824, its cargo included 2000 natural history illustrations, a huge number of plant and animal specimens, and even a live tapir.

He employed, at not insignificant expense, a number of local collectors to search out new items for his collection, as well as artists and mapmakers to record the geography of the islands.

As Lieutenant Governor in Sumatra he was an enthusiastic traveller, often with Sophia in tow, sometimes in arduous conditions. The aims were botanical, scientific and geological. But Raffles also found time to meet and conclude new treaties with some of the local leaders. He was disappointed to find that these were subsequently disavowed by the Company, who felt he was exceeding his mandate.

He communicated widely with other interested individuals, in the region and at home. He sent specimens back to the museums in London, although the contribution would have been much greater had the main collection survived the final journey.

Raffles and his Company could extract business value from his studies. But they could extract even more from an environment in which information could move as freely as he believed trade should be allowed to.

Lesson 3

Make yourself indispensable

Every work group tends to contain a worker who has made themselves indispensable. We all know the type of person. Tasks tend to gravitate towards them, because they invariably know the answer to any question, are always ready to take on new challenges, and consistently deliver results. You begin to get the impression that the whole place would collapse without them. Indispensable workers, however, risk being taken for granted. Sometimes they can even be passed over for promotion, as they are doing such a good job where they are. Becoming indispensable, while at the same time demonstrating eagerness to move on, is a difficult balance to strike. Raffles managed to get it right.

Raffles arrived in Penang in 1805 as the most junior member of the governor's staff, an assistant secretary. There were around a hundred Europeans there: a pretty dull group, more interested in their social life than in learning about their Asian surroundings. It was relatively easy for someone of Raffles' talents and drive to stand out.

He gradually set about making himself indispensable, accreting tasks to himself. He took the minutes of the young colony's council. He deployed his considerable drafting skills to take responsibility for drafting the dispatches back to head office. Showing an early enthusiasm for public relations, which he was to hone so effectively later, he took charge of Penang's newspaper.

Sometimes he displaced others less suited to the task. He was appointed Recorder for the Law Court, over the head of the local magistrate John Dickens, who stormed off to Calcutta in a huff. "With his heart full of rancour and his mouth full of scurrility against [Raffles]", as Olivia put it. This was to become a familiar pattern in Raffles' career: leap-frogging over less talented colleagues, who subsequently pursued vendettas against him.

No one else on the Presidency staff could match his Malay language skills, and soon he became the official translator for correspondence with the local leaders.

Within 18 months of arriving in Penang, he was promoted to Chief Secretary to the Governor. His salary increased by a third to £2,000. Then, as now, success in an expatriate posting could bring financial rewards. He became responsible for shipping, administration, price regulation and disciplinary issues.

But Raffles was too sharp to get stuck in one place for long. He prepared a lengthy report on South East Asian politics, which impressed regional HQ. He travelled back to

Calcutta and persuaded Governor General Minto to appoint him to a special post as Agent in Malacca, reporting directly to Minto, without going through Penang.

Again in Malacca he set about making himself indispensable. He produced a detailed analysis of the numbers and disposition of French and Dutch troops in Java, which proved vital in Minto's subsequent conquest of the Dutch territory. The Navy even looked to him for advice on prevailing wind patterns, to help the fleet steer the most effective course through the archipelago. Raffles had done more than anyone else to plan the invasion: it seemed only fitting that Minto should reward his efforts by placing him in charge of the new British possession.

In Java, and subsequently in Bencoolen, Raffles was running his own show. Bosses invariably like to think they are indispensable. His subordinates didn't always think so.

The key historical and business judgement is whether Raffles was indispensable in the creation of Singapore. The answer has to be an unequivocal yes. Others also played important roles in its subsequent development. Initially there were Scots like Farquhar who Raffles left in charge of Singapore, and Crawford his successor.

There were many other dynamic individuals, expatriate and local, who took the colony forward over the following two centuries. And of course the longest serving CEO, Lee Kuan Yew, who transformed the business model, and took Singapore to new heights of performance in the second half of the 20th century, turning it into a global brand in its own right, not just a multinational subsidiary.

But without Raffles, none of this would have happened. The creation of Singapore was not inevitable. Once the new product had been launched, like all the best ideas, it just seemed that way.

Lesson 4

Spot the market gap and get there fast

In today's fast moving environment, speed to market is essential. The company which spots the market gap, and moves in most swiftly, gains significant advantage. By the time the competitors have piled in, putting pressure on everyone's margins, it is too late. Information did not flow at quite the same speed in Raffles' day. Nevertheless it was still very important to respond quickly to take advantage of new and potential opportunities.

Raffles was not only constantly alert for opportunities around the regional market place, he always strove to get there first and take advantage of them. Nowhere was this more apparent than in his hasty appropriation of Singapore.

Frequently he let his enthusiasm get the better of him. His Company employers were concerned at the ambition and energy he displayed on taking on the governorship of Java, knowing that the island was likely to be returned to the Dutch in due course at the end of the war.

His time in Java was not a commercial success, despite his energetic quest to find new products and reform the economic system (reorganising the supply chains as it would be called today). The main problem was that the war which had brought the British into Java was also closing off the markets of continental Europe.

Some of his schemes were wildly optimistic. He even sent a ship to Japan, then all but closed to the western world, with a trade cargo including an elephant. Of course, like all entrepreneurs, some ideas failed. The elephant had to be returned when the port at Nagasaki proved to have no way of offloading the huge beast.

Nor was his subsequent tenure as Lieutenant Governor of Bencoolen much more successful commercially. It was not promising material. Located in the wrong position, off the main trade routes, its economic infrastructure had been allowed to fall into disrepair, by poor quality, unmotivated and often corrupt managers.

A classic opportunity for a turnaround consultant to restore the operation to financial viability. Raffles certainly tried. But his efforts were ultimately unsuccessful. He tried various export lines, but could not make the economics work.

At one time he was paying four shillings and seven pence for local nutmeg, while the UK market price was just three shillings. By the time he left Sumatra in 1824 there were half a million loss-making coffee trees in his portfolio.

Raffles' reputation then rests much more heavily on the establishment of Singapore and its subsequent commercial success, than on his role as governor in either Java or Sumatra.

He was very conscious that the Dutch ambition was to dominate the Straits so completely as to effectively exclude British merchants from the opportunities in China. The British possessions at Penang and Bencoolen were too far away to be of much use.

His local colleagues and regional head office in Calcutta recognised this too. But they were reluctant to do anything about it for fear of antagonising the Dutch, who had numerical superiority in the region.

Raffles knew he had to move fast to find a weak spot in the competition's position, which could be exploited. The British could not simply leave the market place uncontested. His establishment of a toe-hold, through the new settlement in Singapore, was both visionary and daring. Within a very short space of time, the growth of Singapore had secured a strong market share for Britain.

The reaction of his local bosses was ambivalent. The Governor General in Calcutta wrote: "Your proceedings in establishing a factory at that place do honour to your approved skills and abilities, though the measure itself, as willingly incurring a collision with the Dutch authorities, is to be regretted."

His bosses in London were more unequivocal. They were quick to disown the venture publicly, apologising to the Dutch government for his action in seizing Singapore. Foreign Secretary Castlereagh, writing to the Dutch Ambassador, said: "The acts of Sir Thomas Raffles will be entirely disavowed, that gentleman being merely a commercial agent and not having been authorised to act politically in any manner whatsoever." But privately they offered tacit support, by making clear that total Dutch domination of the eastern trade would not be acceptable.

Canning, another Foreign Secretary, subsequently wrote to Raffles, noting that he had had to express criticism of Raffles for "the freedom with which you committed your government without their knowledge or authority to measures which might have brought a war upon them unprepared." But he added that: "I was not less anxious to retain the fruits of your policy which appeared to be really worth preserving."

Finally the market niche was secured when the Dutch accepted the existence of Singapore, as part of a market sharing deal in 1824, which included brand portfolio swaps – the Dutch giving up Malacca in exchange for Bencoolen.

Raffles had always known he was right about Singapore. As he said in a letter from Bencoolen: "Once the value of Singapore is properly understood, the whole of England will be in its favour."

Lesson 5

Don't be afraid to challenge the received wisdom

Some of the greatest business successes have occurred because an innovator was willing to challenge the conventional wisdom. They said the Sony Walkman and the personal computer would never catch on. Sometimes, of course, the conventional wisdom is right: the annals of business history are also full of heroic failures. But for those who get it right, the potential rewards are enormous.

Those who are most ready to challenge the received wisdom are often outsiders like Raffles. If you are part of the system, with a reasonably comfortable future assured, there is much less incentive to run against the grain. Walking the road less trodden can be a lonely journey, with many unforeseen mishaps along the way, and a crowd of spectators at the other end waiting to say: "I told you so."

If you come up from the bottom, like Raffles, you have nothing to lose. Once he had secured the life-changing opportunity to break away from the humdrum serfdom of clerking in the London offices of the East India Company, and seek his fortune on the other side of the world, he never looked back. He was a man in a hurry. He didn't have time to sit back and go with the flow.

Raffles' whole career is one of challenging the received wisdom. In some cases that received wisdom was based on pretty sketchy information. He was not satisfied with someone else's description of how the East worked. He had to see for himself. Exploring the terrain, researching the history, and getting to know and respect the local people.

Like many a self-educated man, he had the intellectual confidence to question his orders and try to do things differently.

On his second assignment, in Malacca, he was instructed to run down the city to encourage its business to slip away to Penang, before the colony was returned to the Dutch after the Napoleonic wars. Raffles did not think this was the right approach, and set out to prove it with statistics.

He discovered that Penang itself would suffer if the native trade flows centred on Malacca were disrupted. By weight of evidence and power of argument, he persuaded his superiors in Calcutta to change course.

Again in Java, his instructions were essentially to keep things ticking over until the Dutch returned.

But Raffles was the wrong man to put in charge of a holding operation. He defied his orders by seeking to introduce radical administrative reforms within the former Dutch territories, and by seeking new lands which Britain could hold on to when Java was returned to the Dutch.

In Bencoolen too, he sought to expand his fief through new treaties with local leaders. He tried to develop a number of new business ventures, to find profitable opportunities.

But in both cases, departing from his mandate was not to prove commercially successful, and only resulted in reprimands from head office.

By far his most important act of defiance was in establishing Singapore. Raffles knew he was right – Britain had to get a foothold in the Straits or be squeezed out of the China trade by the incumbent Dutch. He believed that, in their hearts, his superiors knew he was right, though they could not condone a strategy which risked provoking a serious reaction from the Dutch.

He went well beyond his orders in signing a treaty and establishing a settlement in Singapore. In the event it was a good call. The Dutch moaned, but did not counter attack.

His bosses criticised him, but quietly allowed Singapore to be reinforced. And the new business unit went from strength to strength. A vindication of his stance in daring to row against the tide.

Of course it was rather easier to defy or misinterpret orders when your regional bosses were several weeks away, and communication with corporate HQ in London could take a year for a single message to go in each direction.

How many expat managers today wish that they were

free of HQ computers interrogating their financial performance even while they sleep, so that they face a slew of emails with new instructions in the morning.

But if you really want to go against the received wisdom, and believe you can make a success of it, the best approach – just as in Raffles' time – is to ensure you have a well-placed mentor at HQ, to cover your back.

Lesson 6

Find a good mentor

Patronage was far more important in Raffles' time than today. Inevitably it tended towards corruption and inefficiency, preventing jobs from being allocated on the basis of merit. Patronage has been phased out in modern corporations, to be replaced by the concept of mentoring. Everyone familiar with large corporate structures will know the value of having a highly placed mentor, or indeed several. Mentors can put their protégé in a place where he will have an opportunity to shine. They can usefully cover his back if things go wrong.

Some writers have suggested that Raffles' original overseas assignment was secured in return for marrying Olivia, and relieving his boss's son of an emotional entanglement with her. Others think that he won Olivia as a result of the posting; she was so enamoured with the prospect of being an expat wife! Certainly they became engaged within days of learning of his posting.

In any case, throughout his career, Raffles proved adept at cultivating and assiduously deploying a series of valuable patrons. This was just as well given his propensity to go against the grain and challenge the accepted wisdom.

The most significant patron was Lord Minto, Scottish nobleman and Governor General of India, and thus of British possessions further east, from 1807. Raffles accompanied Minto on the expedition to take Java in 1811. Minto was so impressed with his energy and enthusiasm, as well as the local expertise which he had so quickly assimilated, that he appointed Raffles Lieutenant Governor of Java, over the heads of several colleagues with more experience.

Minto's support at regional HQ in Calcutta was invaluable to a young man on the distant periphery of empire, always pushing the boundaries, both literally and figuratively. He baled his young protégé out of trouble on a number of occasions.

Raffles used his first visit home in 1816 to cultivate new patrons. The most notable was the Princess Charlotte, daughter of the Prince Regent (later George IV) and thus heir to the throne. He showered her with gifts of oriental curios and developed an active correspondence. Unfortunately she died in childbirth in 1817, depriving Raffles of his most highly placed supporter. Had she survived to become Queen, Raffles could well have ended up as Governor General of India.

When Minto was replaced by Lord Moira in 1813, it

was a major blow to Raffles. He had lost not just his key corporate sponsor, but also a valued ally and sounding board. Raffles could not look to Moira for special preferment when Java was returned to the Dutch in 1816 and he was no longer needed in the colony. Fortunately, Minto had managed to protect his protégé by securing for Raffles in advance the post of Lieutenant Governor of Bencoolen. It was an inferior position to Java, but at least a base from which to pursue his territorial ambitions.

Moira took office with some scepticism about the pushy young turk in Bencoolen. There were many around him in Calcutta who were only too happy to put in a bad word.

Raffles realised he needed to go to see the new boss in person. He seized on an ambiguous phrase in a letter from Calcutta, deliberately misreading it as an invitation to visit. He instantly set sail on the first available vessel, necessitating a perilous voyage on a tiny ship.

But it was a chance well taken. Moira, like others before him, was impressed by Raffles' charm and vitality. He was persuaded by Raffles of the dangers of the Dutch totally excluding English trade from the Straits. He never became a father figure like Minto, but from then on Raffles had his boss's ear. Raffles secured the instructions he so desperately wanted. Indeed he appears to have written the "business plan" himself. He was empowered to explore the Straits to identify possible bases for British trade.

A mentor at HQ was particularly important at a time when communication with regional HQ in Calcutta and corporate HQ in London took many months. The long lead times created a management vacuum which Raffles readily took advantage of, exploiting ruthlessly every ounce of flexibility in his written orders.

Lesson 7

Have a long term vision but pursue it pragmatically

All great business leaders have to be something of a visionary. They have to have the "helicopter" ability to raise their head above the hurly burly of today's market place, to focus on where they want to take the business in the long term. But it is not enough just to be a dreamer. You also have to be able to identify the practical steps to realise that vision, then start taking them. Raffles had all these qualities in good measure. He had the flair of the marketing man, the discipline of the accountant, but above all the visionary drive of the CEO.

We have seen that Raffles could be impetuous at times. Trying to push forward on all fronts at once. Seizing opportunities as they arose. But that did not stop him from having a long term vision of what he wanted to achieve, for himself, for the Company, and for his country's role in the Indies.

As Lieutenant Governor of Java he had clear long term plans for the development of the territory, even though his bosses had indicated that there would be no long term – Java would be handed back to the Dutch in due course.

It was like a modern multinational dispatching a manager to run a joint venture operation with one of its rivals, making clear that the operation would be limited, in duration and geographic extent.

Raffles was determined to tilt the balance in the joint venture relationship. He carefully sought to expand the possessions on the island, with a view to retaining them in the long term – only handing back to the Dutch what had been theirs in the first place.

Raffles could not content himself with being a caretaker manager. Not least because he genuinely believed that there was a better way to run the place. He set in hand a raft of measures to reorganise trade, the legal system and land tenure, as well as to research Java's natural resources.

The Dutch must have greeted him with a mixture of awe and bemusement. They never knew what he was going to ask for next. There is a story that Raffles wrote to one Dutch official to say that his assistant was corrupt and should be suspended. The Dutchman, whose English was poor, looked the word up in the dictionary and promptly had the poor fellow hanged.

In Sumatra too, he displayed vision. He knew Bencoolen was in the wrong place strategically. But that did not stop him trying to boost its critical mass by signing treaties with local chieftains, all of which were immediately disavowed by the Company.

But his real vision was for Singapore. The role it could fulfil as Britain's hub in the vitally important sea lanes to China, and the nature of the place it needed to be to maximise its prospects for long term success.

This combination of long term strategic thinking and short term action can perhaps best be observed in his first week in Singapore. From the first he envisaged a great trading centre. He had the imagination to recognise the long term strategic potential of the location. But that did not stop him drawing up extensive and detailed plans for the administration of the settlement, in a whirlwind of activity over a matter of days. He left poor Farquhar, his deputy, breathless.

When he returned for his third, final and longest visit to Singapore in 1822-23, he threw himself into even more detailed city planning. He drafted laws and regulations, established a system of magistrates, a registry of lands, a college, a botanical garden and his famous residential plan for the town.

It appears that Raffles' vision did not always coincide with that of his superiors. "Lack of goal congruence" as it would be described in modern management-speak. But while they often did not approve of his short term methods, there tended to be a grudging acknowledgement of what he was trying to achieve in terms of Britain's place in the East.

Sometimes results surpass the vision of even the most visionary originators. The achievement that is modern Singapore would have been beyond Raffles' wildest dreams. It would not have been achieved without the dynamism of subsequent leaders, and the energy of the people themselves. But that is not to detract from the contribution of the man who had the original vision back in 1819.

Lesson 8

Sell yourself and your ideas

Raffles was a smart marketeer and a natural salesman – of his ideas, and of himself. His writings, both books and journalism, provided effective advertising copy, aimed at informing and persuading the target audience. In person he seems to have been extremely persuasive.

Raffles was a self-publicist, a relentless self-promoter. He understood the tricks of the public relations business. His writings, although partly driven by a natural curiosity, were certainly also intended as a marketing tool. He aimed to raise awareness in Calcutta and London of the Malay archipelago, of its commercial potential, and of course of Raffles himself.

His return to London from Java, after the colony had been returned to the Dutch, was in part a promotional tour. He wrote the impressive two-volume *History of Java*, which brought him to public prominence, and secured his entry into the salons of the movers and shakers of English society.

He won prestigious quality assurance accreditation: a fellowship in the Royal Society, and a knighthood. What is a knighthood, after all, but an enhancement of your personal branding. The strategy worked well: both he and the region were now on people's radar screens.

Back in Sumatra, he continued to court the press, with a string of high profile articles about his travels around the island.

Raffles understood the concepts of both mass marketing, through channels like the press, and targeted selling. In an early version of customer relationship management (CRM), he corresponded regularly with a wide range of carefully selected key players, whose influence could be helpful. They included people like the Duchess of Somerset.

He was a master of advertising copy. His descriptions of the lands of the Indies were invariably hyperbolic. The land he surveys is always teeming with wildlife, "embosomed in verdure" and with boundless commercial potential. He wrote to his patron, the Duchess of Somerset, on establishing

Singapore, that it was "one of the most safe and extensive harbours in these seas, with every facility for protecting shipping in time of war."

He also understood the need to suppress bad copy. When a disappointed subordinate like Farquhar went into print complaining about his treatment at the hands of Raffles, and claiming credit for having founded Singapore in the first place, there was an instant rebuttal. Raffles leapt into print, refuting the claims.

He also seems to have been particularly impressive in person. Like all good salesmen, he believed that he had only to leap onto a boat and get back to regional HQ in Calcutta, and he would be able to persuade his superiors of his way of thinking. Sometimes he pulled this off very successfully. His bosses found his combination of enthusiasm and practical ability very infectious.

Raffles' self-marketing was not limited to his colleagues and patrons. He seems to have won over the natives wherever he went. The Malayan writer Munshi Abdullah, who chronicled his experiences of Raffles as a young man, describes him as "smiling with infinite charm and nodding his head in deference, his words as sweet as a sea of honey". If only all of our colleagues would say things like this about us.

Friends like Munshi Abdullah, and above all his second wife Sophia, were enthusiastic partners in promoting the Raffles story. Indeed the marketing efforts of Sophia after his death played a vital role in securing Raffles' place in posterity.

Lesson 9

Set smart goals and monitor performance

The process of setting financial performance targets is fundamental to modern business. Woe betide the manager who fails to "deliver on the numbers". But it is also important to set targets for a wider range of performance indicators as criteria for evaluating success. The textbooks say that such objectives should be SMART: Specific, Measurable, Agreed, Realistic and Time-related. These near term targets have to be set within the framework of the long term business goals. Setting clear objectives was particularly important in South East Asia in the early 19th century, when lines of communication were long, and face to face contacts with superiors were separated by long periods of absence.

When Raffles departed from Singapore at the end of his first whirlwind ten-day visit, in February 1819, he issued a proclamation leaving Farquhar in charge. Wouldn't we all like to be able to issue proclamations, instead of mere office memos? He also left a letter of detailed instructions for work to be taken forward in his absence.

This included specific instructions for infrastructure development. He was clearly not expecting to find the market place left uncontested for long, since the priorities he listed included a fort, log-house, batteries, defences and a tower.

When he returned in June for three months, he appraised Farquhar's performance against objectives and, where they fell short, identified the action required. He also recast priorities in the light of developments, which had been fairly dramatic, with the arrival of some 5,000 Chinese in the space of a few months.

Once again he set out a long list of further instructions, before departing Singapore in September. One hesitates to use the word pedantic, but he took pains to cross reference this with his earlier mandate, in order to demonstrate his attention to detail: "I think it necessary to call your particular attention to the eleventh paragraph of my letter of 6 February and the importance of immediately improving the conveniences of the port for shipping, an object to which in the present advanced state of the settlement, all others ought to give way." Substitute email for letter, and this kind of missive from the boss would be familiar to all of us.

When he returned three years later, he was somewhat disappointed with Farquhar's failure to deliver on a number of these objectives. So he sacked him and appointed Crawford.

When Raffles finally left Singapore for the last time, in

June 1823, he once again issued a departing letter of instructions to Crawford. It even included advice on handling the petty snobbisms of colonial society: "The peace of small settlements being frequently disturbed by disputes concerning rank, particularly of the ladies, I think it would be advisable for you to avoid fixing any real rank whatsoever." Sound advice indeed.

Today, progress on objectives tends to be assessed at fixed intervals, with quarterly and annual reporting cycles. In Raffles' time it was a more haphazard process. Progress reports could be forwarded to regional HQ in Calcutta and corporate HQ in London, but the long transmission times by sea meant that feedback took months. Detailed appraisals tended to take place mainly when the boss was next passing through.

In the case of Singapore, ill health and family tragedies meant that Raffles was away for over three years between his second and third visits. This can't have made it easy to chase progress on objectives. Hardly surprising then that he returned to find some of his instructions had been modified by Farquhar in the light of local circumstances.

Lesson 10

Set clear reporting lines

Clear reporting lines are important for the effective functioning of any large organisation. Ambiguity and confusion can make control difficult. But modern multinationals increasingly function as "matrix organisations", with overlapping reporting lines drawn up on the basis of geography, business area and function. Management hierarchies are kept as flat as possible. This would be very difficult to do without the kind of information flows which are permitted by modern IT. The East India Company tended to be much more hierarchical. Nevertheless, restless local CEOs like Raffles found ways of subverting command chains by going direct to senior corporate management over the heads of immediate superiors. There was always plenty of scope for local autonomy.

When Raffles first arrived in the East, he was working for the governor of the newly established Presidency of Penang. Malacca, his next posting, also came under the supervision of Penang. But the thrusting newcomer was always striving to get noticed by regional HQ in Calcutta.

He finally won control of his own territory when he was appointed Lieutenant Governor of Java, and subsequently of Bencoolen. Much of the problem with his military commander Gillespie in Java could be ascribed to lack of goal congruence between the geographical and functional models of management. Raffles saw himself in charge of everything that happened on the island. Gillespie, as military commander, saw himself as part of a different command chain.

Not surprisingly, after establishing Singapore, Raffles attached great importance to being allowed to continue to supervise it from Bencoolen. Equally unsurprisingly, his territorial rival in Penang contested this.

Regional HQ came down in favour of Raffles, not least because of the somewhat different business models being adopted in the two markets. Raffles' commercial policy strongly emphasised Singapore's free port status. Raffles ran a lean mean operation in Singapore, with initially just three or four British officials, compared with over two dozen in Penang.

Raffles established a series of financial controls for Singapore. He instructed Farquhar to keep: "an account particular of military disbursements", "a general account particular of every disbursement", and "a general treasury account" showing monthly balances of expenditure against receipts.

This became a subject of fierce dispute between the two. Farquhar believed that he should submit the accounts direct to regional HQ in Calcutta. Raffles insisted that they were to be forwarded by way of Bencoolen. It was the beginning of the end for Farquhar.

When Raffles left Singapore in the hands of its new Resident, Crawford, Calcutta decided to take direct control over the new settlement.

As long ago as 1819, Raffles had proposed that all three Straits settlements – Singapore, Malacca and Penang – should be brought under one command. No prizes for guessing who he had in mind to take on this important role. And that is indeed what eventually happened, but it came too late for Raffles.

Lesson 11

Work with the market

The East India Company was a regulated monopoly. This is a cosy situation to be in, which many business managers would envy. But it can be a disincentive to innovation, and does not necessarily promote the most efficient use of resources. The issue of Free Trade was a major political controversy in the UK at the time. Raffles' views on the subject were clear: he saw that Singapore's future prosperity rested on making it a free port, open to the world's trade.

The Napoleonic wars in Europe had the effect of barring Continental markets to British goods. At the same time, British traders had a virtual monopoly of trade elsewhere, backed by the global dominance of the Royal Navy. American businessmen were irate at being kept out of European markets by the British blockade. This tension spilled over into a second Anglo-US conflict, "the War of 1812", only 30 years after the two countries had fought a bloody war of independence.

Meanwhile, the Anglo-French conflict caused huge fluctuations in trade, prices and employment which periodically led to extremes of poverty and starvation among both urban and rural poor in England. After victory at Waterloo, when the price of corn collapsed, the British Parliament, dominated by the landed gentry, passed the 1815 Corn Law to protect domestic farmers at the expense of consumers. This measure which set the rural against the urban interest was a subject of fierce controversy for 30 years, until it was finally repealed in 1846.

Well before this, Huskisson – President of the Board of Trade – had begun to reform the messy patchwork of tariffs which, for a combination of revenue-raising and protectionist purposes, distorted trade grievously. In 1823, when Raffles' time in the East was drawing to a close, Huskisson started to tackle the Navigation Acts, which for a century and a half had given British shippers monopolistic privileges in British ports.

The free market policies advocated by Adam Smith were gaining increasing sway in Britain. The first country to benefit from the advances of the industrial revolution, its manufacturing exporters had much to gain from minimising the costs of their raw material inputs and maximising the overseas markets for their products.

Raffles believed in the market place. His approach as Lieutenant Governor of Java was very different from that of its former colonial masters the Dutch. The Dutch had operated a mercantilist policy: directing the peasants on what to grow, then acting as monopoly purchaser of the entire output at suppressed prices for export to Holland.

Raffles tried to introduce a more liberal regime, in which the peasants could sell their goods on the open market. Unfortunately his enlightened policy proved expensive, causing the Administration in Java to continue to rely on Calcutta for subsidies. Not at all what they had intended.

He was also an advocate of free trade. On founding Singapore he had said: "Our object is not territory, but trade." He recognised that for Singapore to flourish amidst competition from the Dutch territories in South East Asia, and in order to attract the small Chinese, Malay and Bugis traders, it had to be a free port.

The formula proved successful from the start. Traders flocked into the new port, to take advantage of its free trade status. Shipping volumes grew rapidly. It never looked back. These policies have been pursued by Singaporean leaders right up to the present day. Their fruits are obvious to any casual observer of Singapore's port in the 21st century – still the second busiest in the world.

Lesson 12

Build wider stakeholder relationships

Who is a business run for? Its owners? Its managers? Its employees? They all have a legitimate interest in the way a company is run. But so too do a number of other stakeholders: the customers, the suppliers, and the societies in which it operates. Modern corporations understand the importance of building relationships with this wide array of stakeholders. To some extent they are required to do so by laws and regulations. But the most effective companies realise that going beyond the minimum requirements can actually deliver competitive advantages to their operations. Raffles was an early proponent of the stakeholder interest.

Raffles certainly courted the owners' interest assiduously. He sought to secure influence and patronage in London. He also worked hard to keep senior managers on-side. He was fairly successful, particularly in his relationships with his immediate bosses in Calcutta, which allowed him to get away with some daring entrepreneurial behaviour.

But ultimately his willingness to play it fast and loose with corporate guidelines lost him the support of the Company hierarchy, which was to prove so disastrous at the end of his career.

His relationships with employee stakeholders were also mixed. He commanded a mixture of loyalty and hatred in almost equal measure.

But it was among the external stakeholder groups that Raffles operated most effectively. From his earliest days in Penang and Malacca, he went to great pains to develop strong links with local Malay leaders. He travelled widely to meet them. He kept up a steady stream of correspondence through which he gained their goodwill by presents and "agreeable words".

He understood well the importance of personal relationships in Asian culture. He learned how to show appropriate deference and use gifts to build mutual obligations. But perhaps most importantly, he showed genuine respect for the local people at a time when many western colonialists foolishly held them in contempt.

In Java, imposed on the reluctant Dutch settlers as their temporary commander-in-chief, he tried to build relationships with the former colonial masters. In part he needed to do this to make the system work. In part he recognised that he had much to learn from their experience of the local political and economic scene. But in part it was also in his nature to seek to cooperate with other stakeholders.

He won their respect, and in some cases their friendship. But subsequent Dutch historians of this period have often been much more critical of Raffles than British ones, tending to portray him as corrupt and rapacious. Perhaps that is not surprising, for without Raffles and the rise to prominence of Singapore, who knows how different the colonial history of South East Asia might have been.

When he established the settlement in Singapore, in contradiction of his orders, and in the teeth of opposition from other parts of his organisation including his rival in Penang, he realised the importance of securing backing from other stakeholders.

One such group was the business community in Calcutta, who stood to gain significantly from a better toe-hold into the China trade through the Straits. His network of personal contacts, and careful work with the media, ensured that his exploits received favourable coverage in the Calcutta press.

Raffles also worked closely with a broad array of scientists and scholars who had a stake in the Company's increasing presence in the Indies, because of the huge new fields of scientific discovery which it opened up.

Lesson 13

Be a good corporate citizen

Business academics talk about "environmental marketing" – selling the company not just through its products and services, but also by how it is generally perceived by others. A reputation as a good corporate citizen can help a company's marketing efforts. A reputation as a bad one can damage a brand – as we have seen with major multinationals which have been criticised for polluting the environment or employing sweatshop labour. A good reputation can also be an important asset in recruiting top quality staff. Most people want to work for an organisation they can feel proud of.

Raffles was commercially driven. He wanted to secure new markets for the Company, at the expense of its competitors. He wanted to make profits for the Company and for himself. But he was interested in more than just profits. He genuinely cared about the well-being of his colonies and their inhabitants.

Throughout his time in the East he was a determined opponent of slavery. The British Parliament had voted to ban the slave trade in 1807, thanks to the efforts of Wilberforce, a cross-bench Member of Parliament from Yorkshire, and in the face of opposition from shipping interests in Liverpool and Bristol.

Then began the long campaign to eradicate slavery throughout the Empire. It was one of the first modern political campaigns using new lobbying techniques to persuade public opinion, and drawing heavily on the evangelical and dissenting church movements which were growing in importance in England. But it was a hard fight, against strong vested interests in the West Indies colonies, and did not finally succeed until 1833.

Raffles met Wilberforce in 1817 in London, and they became good friends, regular correspondents and, later in retirement, neighbours in Hendon.

When Raffles was appointed Lieutenant Governor of Java in 1811, he was determined to eradicate slavery there. He struggled to achieve it by manipulating the prevailing Dutch laws. Subsequently in Bencoolen, he freed the few hundred African slaves, wrote off their debts and established a school for them. He tried to rehabilitate the convict workers, who had been shipped from Bengal, encouraging them to marry and become proper citizens.

He was opposed to the opium business, although this

was more difficult as it was such an important commodity for the Company. Nevertheless he was able to achieve significant reductions in usage in Java. When Farquhar proposed establishing opium shops in the new territory of Singapore, Raffles rejected the idea. That didn't stop Farquhar going ahead – yet another source of disagreement between the two.

He sought to severely restrict the spread of gambling, which he had witnessed driving people into debt and poverty. He also abolished the use of torture in Java.

His plans for Singapore were not restricted solely to the commercial. He dabbled in urban planning, drawing up detailed ideas for the civil administration, residential areas for the various races, and amenities such as a botanical garden and the Plain, now the Padang.

At the end of his life back in London, even when burdened by ill health and enmeshed in bitter disputes with his former employers, he still found time to be one of the major movers in the setting up of London Zoo.

Lesson 14

Know when to put on a show

Extravagant display and entertainment on a grand scale can be a feature of corporate life, particularly in Asia. Companies sponsor major sporting and artistic events, and often celebrate anniversaries with spectacular parties. Sometimes this is criticised as capitalist excess, particularly by lower paid workers. But there may be a number of business justifications. For a young, fast-growing company, it is a way of demonstrating that it has arrived, and of attracting attention. In the services sector, where the product may be intangible, public display may help to promote an impression of substance to support both sales and the share price. And of course, inviting customers and other stakeholders to enjoyable events is an important part of relationship building. Raffles understood these marketing tools well.

From his early days in Penang, Raffles recognised the importance of entertaining. With the help of Olivia, his house became a key social centre in the colony.

His hospitality became even more grand on assuming the governorship of Java. He moved into the elegant mansion of the former Dutch Governor General at Buitenzorg, a short distance from Batavia. Such public display was important to demonstrate that the island was now under new, British, management. But the parties were also a valuable opportunity to get alongside leading players from the Dutch and Javanese communities. Raffles knew he had to work with these people, and as far as possible he aimed to make them friends too.

His sense of status stood Raffles in good stead when paying an introductory call on the Sultan of Yogyakarta in 1811. The Sultan tried to stage manage the meeting to put himself at an advantage, by placing Raffles in an inferior seating position. It was a tense moment. Raffles' entourage was heavily outnumbered: any sign of weakness would have been an invitation to the Sultan to attack him. But Raffles was not one to be upstaged. With calm dignity, he refused to sit until the room had been rearranged to his liking. The Sultan's bluff was called, and the event passed off without further incident.

Back in London for his long leave, Raffles was determined to cut a dash. He rented a large house at a posh address in the West End, and hired a bevy of retainers as well as a carriage and splendidly bedecked grooms.

He had come a long way from the poor clerk who had left England just over a decade before. And he wanted to show it. He intended to move in the grandest circles, and he used his new wealth to match the style of his new aristocratic acquaintances. Of course, style alone would not be enough.

It got him through the door of the smart salons, but it was his intellectual weight, his commercial and political acumen, and his not inconsiderable charm which made him welcome there.

Back in the East, he demonstrated the importance of symbolism to seal a deal, when staging the signing of his Singapore treaty with the Sultan of Johor. He set up tents and a red carpet and had all the ship's officers come ashore in full dress uniform. Gun salutes were fired, toasts were drunk and the corporate trade mark – the Union Jack flag – was much in display.

So there was sound business sense in Raffles' public style. As well, of course, as the natural ebullience of the self-made entrepreneur. But it must have made some people resentful, and it no doubt contributed to the long running series of allegations from the Company that he must have been fiddling his expenses.

For most of us, the standard rule of thumb tends to be that corporate events to which we are personally invited are a sound business investment, while those from which we are excluded are a profligate waste of the shareholders' money.

Lesson 15

Create teams not enemies

"Team working" has become a buzz word. But successful organisations have long recognised the importance of effective teams, whose product is more than the sum of the parts. Great attention is placed on putting together teams with the right combination of skill sets and personality traits. Good managers do not have to be popular. But they have to be able to get their teams to deliver the right results. In some ways, Raffles was an effective manager of human resources. But it was an area in which he also had conspicuous failings.

For all his ability to charm senior mentors and build around him effective teams of young acolytes, Raffles was singularly unsuccessful in his relationships with the lieutenants serving directly under him. People seemed to love or hate him. There was nothing in between.

Of course we all like to think we could do our immediate boss's job better than them, given half the chance. No doubt Raffles' subordinates felt this too. This wasn't helped by the fact that they were often older and more experienced, and had been passed over to make way for him. Raffles somehow often managed to turn his staff's attitudes from simmering resentment to deep-seated enmity, with devastating long term consequences for him.

When he won his first command as Lieutenant Governor of Java, he was given Colonel Gillespie as his military commander. Gillespie, an upper-class soldier of Irish extraction, was not a natural soul mate. His military leadership had secured Java for Britain, and he had hoped to be appointed as military governor, so he was bitterly disappointed to see a civil administration put in place, with Raffles in charge. Gillespie resented civilian interference in military disciplines, particularly on budgetary matters. Some things don't change.

Raffles proposed reducing the military garrison to save money. Gillespie objected furiously. Matters between the two of them became so bad that in 1813 he left for Calcutta. He did his utmost to cause trouble for Raffles there, accusing him of improprieties in sales of government land. These allegations were seized on by the new Governor General, already concerned about Raffles' continuing failure to make Java pay. Raffles survived the subsequent lengthy investigation, but it left him permanently damaged.

Raffles also had trouble with Bannerman, Lieutenant Governor in Penang. In part this was the natural rivalry between two neighbouring sales managers, over which of them gets to take on additional territory. But Bannerman genuinely believed that the hot-headed Raffles risked plunging the Straits into a new conflagration with the Dutch, by his precipitate action in establishing a settlement at Singapore. So much so that he refused to send military reinforcements to support it. A decision for which he was subsequently rebuked by Calcutta.

But Raffles' greatest nemesis was the man he left in charge of Singapore, when he departed after his first whirlwind week there. Colonel William Farquhar, seven years older than Raffles, was an ex-soldier and civil servant, with whom he had already worked in Malacca.

When Raffles returned to Singapore for his third, final and longest stay in October 1822, he found the City had made considerable progress. The population had grown to 10,000, of whom only 70 were Europeans, and trade was up to $8.5 million in just three years. But he was a little disappointed with his nominee.

Raffles felt that Farquhar had failed to follow his instructions sufficiently closely in a number of areas. For example, on land usage Farquhar had allowed merchants to settle on the land north of the Singapore River, which was supposed to be reserved for government buildings. He had also permitted opium farms and gambling dens in order to raise revenue.

Raffles complained to Calcutta: "I consider Col Farquhar to be totally unequal to the charge of such an important and peculiar a charge as that of Singapore has now become." While Raffles was metaphorically stabbing him in the back, poor Farquhar was literally stabbed in the front by a local Malay who had run amok after being imprisoned for debt. He recovered, but the two men continued to co-exist uneasily.

To Raffles' disgust, Farquhar had adopted the native style of dress. The final straw came one day when he turned up at an official function in a sarong. This was a long time before footballer David Beckham made them acceptable male attire. Raffles removed him from his duties in May 1823. Several writers have suggested that the clothes issue was actually a proxy for Raffles' distaste at the fact that Farquhar had taken up with a native wife who had borne him children. Fortunately, today's expat managers live in a more enlightened environment.

Farquhar was no doubt more ponderous and less imaginative than Raffles. Perhaps this was what was needed. What small colony could have housed two Raffles? But Farquhar seems to have done a pretty competent job, winning the respect of his local and foreign citizens, and overseeing remarkable growth.

He had arrived in Singapore with only three weeks supplies, and not long afterwards the island was overrun with a plague of rats. Then his dog was eaten by a crocodile. But he persevered and saw significant progress, as well as achieving great popularity among his citizenry. When Farquhar finally left Singapore, he was given a much bigger send off than Raffles, with thousands of people lining the streets.

The furore engendered by his dismissal and Raffles' "flagrant injustice and tyranny" as he saw it, was to become an all-consuming passion for Farquhar. He spent his remaining years in protracted correspondence with the Board of the East India Company creating trouble, and providing much ammunition for Raffles' enemies to use against him. As the saying goes: Be nice to people on the way up – you may need them on the way back down.

Lesson 16

Respect local cultures

Global multinational corporations aim to be at home wherever they operate in the world. While retaining a set of core company values, they recognise the need to be sensitive to local cultures. For successful operation it is essential to understand cultural influences on your employees, your customers and the general business environment. Raffles showed a great deal of interest in and respect for local culture. His first attempts at town planning in the new colony of Singapore showed an understanding of the wide variety of ethnic groups who have played such a key role in building up the City State as a global commercial hub.

Everyone is an individual. One should not over generalise. But it is possible to discern common characteristics within different cultural groups. Contrasts may be drawn, for example, between the individualism of the West and the more group-oriented cultures of the East.

A series of Asian cultural characteristics with specific relevance to business has been identified by business academics. These include virtues like respect for elders and seniors, persistence and thrift, as well as the concept of shame. They tend to show themselves in the way Asian individuals and organisations demonstrate a respect for traditions, place high value on stability and avoiding the loss of face. The concept of mutual duties and obligations may be manifested by the reciprocal exchange of gifts; in some cases these have needed careful policing to avoid turning into cartels.

During the 1980s and 1990s, such Asian values were often held to be superior to the western model, reflecting the economic miracle of Asian tigers like Singapore. Since the financial crisis of the late 90s, cultural ascendancy has been more muted. There is more of a recognition that no one group has got it completely right.

We have seen that Raffles devoted much attention to studying local, particularly Malay, culture. He was also acutely conscious that the success of the new colony depended on its ability to attract significant numbers of commercially driven Chinese entrepreneurs and workers.

In the very earliest days of Singapore, three key ethnic groups dominated the new colony.

The European administrators and merchants were very few in number, and always remained in a small minority.

The Malay community initially consisted primarily of the

Temenggong and his family and camp followers, who had previously occupied themselves mainly with piracy, but were now effectively a rentier class living off the annual stipend paid by the British. Later, a new group of more entrepreneurial Malays moved down from Malacca to take up various occupations. But then, as now, Singapore was basically a Chinese city.

Within six months of Raffles establishing Singapore, some 5,000 Chinese had moved in. They included Peranakans, or Straits Chinese, who had already been living in South East Asia for generations and were heavily intermarried with the locals, as well as direct migrants from China's southern provinces. They spoke a variety of regional dialects. Many provided the labour for the docks and the new agricultural plantations. Others were the entrepreneurial merchants and traders who provided the base for Singapore's rapid transformation into a commercial hub.

There were smaller communities too: Indian soldiers and followers brought over with the British, Bugis traders, Arab merchants, and a small but growing community of Eurasians.

Raffles' town plan for Singapore recognised these different communities by allocating specific areas for them. He made serious attempts to understand the different cultures. He recognised that each group brought its own talents and had its own contribution to make to the future success of the new colony.

There must have been times during his quarrels with Farquhar when Raffles wondered whether it was the Scots who were the most difficult culture to work with. But he was surrounded by them. Scots were the backbone of the East India Company. His bosses, Minto and Moira, were both

Scottish, and when he had to pick a successor for Farquhar, whom should he choose but yet another Scot, John Crawford.

At its most simple level, it is important to get the daily etiquette right in dealing with people from different cultural backgrounds. One should avoid inadvertently serving food which is taboo to the religion of one's guests. Or upsetting a Chinese by wearing the wrong colour or using an unlucky number, or a Malay by an inappropriate physical gesture.

Today's international manager can simply buy a book on local etiquette from his bookstore. But Raffles was starting from scratch. He had to painstakingly figure out how the different communities he encountered worked. He was successful not just because he worked hard at it, but because he approached the process with a genuine sense of respect for different cultures.

It is a lesson which has been well taken by today's managers of Singapore Inc. They have devoted considerable effort to promoting harmonious relations between the various ethnic communities which make up the polyglot multicultural society, from which Singapore draws so much strength. They have been highly successful.

In turn, they have shown respect to Raffles. The arch colonialist, he still finds honour in post colonial Singapore. His name is everywhere. His statues watch over the city. To win that kind of respect, you have to have shown respect in the first place.

Lesson 17

Speak the customer's language

"Think global, act local" is a common mantra of today's multinationals. An important aspect of acting local is the ability to communicate in the language of wherever you are operating. As the old marketing adage goes: "When you're buying, you can speak your own language. When you're selling, speak the customer's". Raffles' Malay language skills were an important part of his personal competitive advantage during his time in the East. That is why he worked so hard on them, both on the journey out to the Indies, and indeed once he got there.

One of the first things business executives do when given their new expatriate posting is to purchase a phrase book and a CD set of language lessons. Some stick at it. You see them engrossed in their headphones on the plane, endlessly repeating banal phrases.

Others, particularly English speakers, are content to rest on the belief that their own language is the lingua franca of global business, and there is little to be served by venturing to learn another.

Being able to work in the local language brings a number of advantages.

It gives you access to the locals. Not just to the thin veneer of intermediaries who have mastered your language, and who may be adjusting their message to suit your sensitivities. But to the domestic players as well, who may well be the real power brokers.

The ability to read a language gives you access to the collective knowledge of that culture. For Raffles, the Malay language was not just a means of communication, but an important field of study in its own right. He even wrote a dictionary, and he collected and studied Malay texts covering many areas of knowledge.

Learning a language very different from one's own is not just about learning a new vocabulary. The student inevitably also learns about the underlying culture and social norms, and the way of thinking which governs how people choose to express themselves, both verbally and through body language.

The locals were very impressed with the way Raffles steeped himself in their culture and language, and they enthusiastically helped him search out and accumulate his collection of manuscripts.

Knowing the local language also gives you an edge over competitors who don't speak it. From his earliest days in Malacca, Raffles made a favourable impression by standing out from the crowd.

So limited was the level of popular education at that time, that some of his compatriots in the East would have been unable to read or write their own language, let alone learn a foreign one. Two centuries later, the language skills of its polyglot, multi-ethnic population are a key component of Singapore's global competitive advantage.

Knowing Malay also increased his credibility with seniors in Calcutta and London. If you respect someone's language skills and local knowledge, you are more likely to respect their judgement on local issues.

However it is always a delicate balance for the expatriate manager, who risks being seen as having "gone native" if he too frequently demonstrates his ability to see issues through the eyes of his host country.

Of course, the quickest way to learn a foreign language is by hooking up with a local partner. Unlike the English, the Dutch were much less inclined to take wives with them from home, and frequently married natives. When Governor Minto first visited Java, he was shocked to find most of the local "society" females only able to converse in Malay.

Some of Raffles' British colleagues, notably Farquhar, did enter into long-lasting relationships with local women. But, as we have seen, Raffles disapproved.

Lesson 18

Have a supportive spouse

Human resource managers say that one of the most important factors for success in an expatriate posting is the extent to which the executive's spouse and family settle comfortably into the new environment. Raffles was very fortunate in the support he received from his two wives, Olivia and Sophia. The East Indies was a difficult and unhealthy place for European women in the early 19th century. Indeed, it killed Olivia, who thus literally gave her life for her husband's career.

Olivia was ten years older than Raffles. Born in India and brought up in Ireland, like many young women of her class and time, she was sent out to India aged 21 to find a husband. En route she became pregnant by the ship's captain, a scandal which was to linger over her in future years in the Far East. She married a surgeon in India, but was widowed at 29 and returned to England, where she apparently met Raffles while pursuing a pension from the East India Company.

It was a whirlwind romance. They were married within five days of the announcement of Raffles' appointment in Penang. Perhaps the allure of an expatriate lifestyle was as strong then as now!

There were rumours that Olivia was somehow instrumental in helping him secure the post, which Raffles always strenuously denied. One suggestion is that Raffles' first patron in the Company, William Ramsay, dispatched them to the Indies to keep Olivia away from his own son, Raffles' close friend. But this ignores the very high opinion of Raffles' talents which Ramsay was known to hold.

Throughout his career, Raffles was invariably accompanied by members of his extended family, as companions and staff. His sister Maryanne joined the party for Penang. Two other sisters followed later.

It cannot have been easy for Olivia in the small, stultifying society of Penang, with rumours circulating about her "scandalous" past. But she threw herself into the role of hostess, organising glittering parties to support her husband's ambitions.

There are differing accounts of the extent of her beauty. But Olivia was clearly a striking figure. "Tall and showy" with an exotic dress sense, she towered over the

Raffles. She was also known to be fond of a drink.

Olivia understood the importance of Raffles developing intellectual ballast to support his career ambitions. She told a friend she was keen to see him complete his book on Malay laws "for the weight that this would give him in the settling of Java".

She also assiduously courted his superiors. From Java she wrote to Governor General Minto in Calcutta: "I…can only assure you in the simple language of the heart that it throbs with affection as dear and as tender for you as ever a child's did for a father." Well, we've all tried to get our partners to write letters like that to the boss haven't we!

The adverse climate of the tropics eventually proved too much for Olivia. She died in 1814 at the age of 43, after nine very happy years of marriage.

Raffles met his second wife, Sophia, while on home leave in England in 1816, and they were married six months later. Within a few months she became Lady Raffles, when he was knighted on 29 May 1817. Five years younger than Raffles, her family was comfortably off thanks to her father's profitable years in India.

Sophia gave birth to their first child, Charlotte, en route back to the East. Like Raffles himself, she was born at sea.

As usual, Raffles gathered family around him. Sophia's brother, William Hull, joined them for the voyage to Bencoolen. He was subsequently replaced by another brother, Robert Hull, and later still her youngest brother, Lawrence Hull, came from Bengal to be Raffles' secretary. Raffles' sister Maryanne also spent some time with them in Bencoolen before joining her husband Captain William Flint in Singapore in 1819, where he had been appointed Master Attendant and Storekeeper of the new settlement.

Sophia, like Olivia, was determined to actively support Raffles' career. She quickly became fluent in Malay. She put up with extraordinary hardships, which most western ladies of her time would not have countenanced, to accompany Raffles on a major fact-finding mission around Sumatra.

At first, family life in Bencoolen was blissful, with Sophia producing three more children there and supporting Raffles in his work and study. But in a matter of months in 1821-22, they lost three of the four children, and several other members of their entourage, to fever. Raffles himself was very unwell and had to be nursed through blinding headaches. The remaining child, Ella, was packed off to England for her health. The following year Sophia had her fifth child, Flora, but the infant died a couple of months later.

Raffles and Sophia finally sailed for home in 1824, arriving in August. The remaining two years of his life were difficult ones, beset with poor health and financial difficulties. They led a fairly quiet life in Hendon, where Raffles died of a massive hemorrhage to his brain tumour on 5 July 1826, the day before his 45th birthday.

Of course, a spouse can support their partner in death as in life. Sophia was determined to redeem Raffles' reputation. She wrote her *Memoir* of Raffles, publishing it in 1830 at her own expense, describing his life and work in the East. This had a significant impact in reforming his reputation.

She also employed, at significant cost to her small remaining funds, an eminent sculptor, Sir Francis Chantrey, to produce a life size statue of Raffles in marble. She was able to lobby successfully to have this installed in Westminster Abbey.

Sophia lived on for another 32 years, dying in 1858. She had had a hard time, constantly struggling with financial difficulties, and devastated by the loss of their remaining child at the age of 19 in 1840. But at least she had the consolation of living to see Raffles' reputation vindicated with the growing success of Singapore.

The biographer of Raffles' wives has suggested that Raffles probably loved Olivia the more deeply. Perhaps Sophia shared this assessment, with some jealousy, because she effectively airbrushes Olivia out of his life in her book. There is just one reference to the first marriage, and that in a footnote, not the main body of the text.

Lesson 19

Make sure the numbers add up

Cash flow is the lifeblood of a business. There are many examples of businesses trading profitably, but which are forced to close after running into cash flow problems. Many an entrepreneur has been frustrated by his accountant's conservatism and relentless pressure on cutting costs. The financial results may be unwelcome, the numbers may lack romance, but they are an acid test of whether the business activity makes sense or not.

Raffles wanted to run a successful business unit. But profit was not his only objective. He had a grander vision. His vision for Singapore was to become "a great commercial emporium", not to become "an efficient profit centre generating maximum Economic Value Added".

He had strong views about the way business should be conducted. He was against slavery and gambling, even though these were promising potential business lines.

Raffles was always more driven by the revenue than the cost side of the P&L account. He was never one to focus on cost-cutting or drawing in of horns. He carried a substantial overhead in the team of family members he kept on his pay roll, as well as his Malay secretariat and the staff he employed to support his scientific researches. Of course Raffles would have seen these as investments rather than costs. But the connection between this expenditure and revenue flows was somewhat loose.

None of his major responsibilities led to great profit. Neither Java nor Bencoolen were particularly successful financially under his governorship. This was not entirely his fault: he was not dealt a strong hand in terms of the underlying economics or the prevailing business climate. But Raffles was more concerned to spend to grow his way out of the problem, rather than batten down the hatches, cut costs and ride out the storm.

Like all the Company employees, Raffles was, of course, concerned to make money for himself. He could achieve none of the great things he intended without it.

When he returned to London in 1816, his financial position had been transformed from that of the penniless clerk who had headed East a decade before. He was able to hire smart rooms, travel and entertain in a manner which cut something of a dash in London society. His new found wealth was a necessary prop to the social progress which he made, including his knighthood.

Where did the money come from? It is difficult to track precisely. Certainly it was well beyond his salary. It clearly reflected a combination of trading on his own account and land speculation. Raffles was able to use his position as governor to influence land allocations. He could see where property values were going to rise, and invest profitably in the land.

It is more easy to say where the money went. Raffles managed to lose most of it in a series of calamities at the end of his career.

As we have seen, Raffles' pension entitlements did not work out quite as he might have hoped. Far from paying him a nice allowance, the Company alleged that he had fiddled his expenses. Specifically they were concerned that he had drawn full pay during the period when he had been on home leave in 1816-17. There were also allegations, dating from his time in Java, of corrupt practices in the sale of government land, for which Raffles himself had been a buyer. In total, they demanded over £20,000 from him.

This was a festering sore for the remainder of Raffles' short life, forced to live in much straitened circumstances, albeit in a pleasant property in Hendon, which he had acquired in 1825.

Eventually Sophia brought the matter to closure with a payment to the Company of £10,000 compensation, leaving her very little to live on.

Lesson 20

Watch the work-life balance - is it all worth it?

Human resource management textbooks today make great play of the work-life balance. Successful managers struggle to make time for their families and personal interests. The financial rewards for wholehearted dedication to the corporate world can be great. But so can the costs. It is a personal cost benefit analysis which we all have to calibrate individually.

For Raffles the personal costs were heavy, and the rewards in his lifetime less than anticipated. The oppressive climate and health hazards of life out East took a devastating toll. He lost his first wife, four of his five children, and died at only 45 of a brain tumour, to which his workaholic nature may well have contributed.

When his fourth child was born in Bencoolen in 1822, he wrote: "I have seen enough of power and wealth to know that, however agreeable to the propensities of our nature, there is more real happiness in domestic quiet and repose, when blessed with a competence, than in all the fancied enjoyments of the great and rich." Very soon, after losing three children in the space of six months in Bencoolen, he sent in his resignation.

He had always been more of an entrepreneur than a company man. But he could not have expected to be so badly treated in retirement. Far from the pension to which he assumed he was entitled, the East India Company argued that he owed them money. They demanded that he return all the salary he had drawn during his mid-tour leave in England, and they sought to claw back other payments relating to land deals.

He suffered significant losses when the *Fame* went down, and was further devastated financially by the collapse of a bank where much of his savings were deposited, and a further sinking of a vessel containing more of his valuables.

During those last months in relatively impoverished retirement in Hendon, suffering agonies from his head pains, did he look back and judge himself a success? Did he feel he had played the corporate game as well as he could? Well, perhaps not then.

But if he could have come forward two centuries, to see what his creation – Singapore – has turned into, in his own words "a great emporium in the East", perhaps he might feel vindicated. His foresight and entrepreneurial drive were ultimately successful beyond his wildest dreams.